The Echo of the School

Eduardo García Romero

The Echo of the School

Copyright © 2024 Eduardo García Romero

ISBN: 9798301842344

DEDICATION

To my dear students, whose curiosity and bravery inspire me every day to explore new mysteries and discover new stories. Thank you for making the classroom a place full of questions, dreams, and learning.

To my family, for their unconditional love and constant support, giving me the strength to keep creating.

To my children, whose boundless imagination reminds me of the magic of seeing the world through curious eyes.

This book is for all of you, who accompany me in every chapter of life, making each story meaningful.
With all my love.

CONTENTS

INDEX

The Echo of the School

Prologue: The Mystery of the School

There are places in the world where time seems to have stopped, where the shadows are longer, and the walls whisper secrets no one dares to hear. Mariana's school is one of those places. Ancient, imposing, and marked by a past that has never been fully unveiled, it is a place where the echoes of history resonate, sometimes eerily. In this place, where the present and the past intertwine in ways that defy logic, the memories of those who are no longer alive remain in some mysterious way.

The story you are about to read does not begin with extraordinary events or obvious tragedy but with something much subtler: a feeling of unease. The sound of a rocking chair moving on its own, a whisper in the dark, an old key forgotten in a dusty room. But what starts as something small soon grows into something much bigger, something that the children of Mariana's school never imagined they would face.

While investigating a series of inexplicable disappearances, and discovering an old link to an orphanage from generations ago, the hidden secrets in the shadows of the school begin to take shape. At the center of it all is Anastasia, a girl whose fate was trapped in a nightmare from which she never awoke. But Anastasia is not the only prisoner of the past. The school, with its history of loss and forgetfulness, harbors something darker and more dangerous than any lost soul.

This is a journey into the unknown, a path crossed by children guided by clues and inexplicable presences, leading them to confront not only the shadows of the past but the dark secrets of those around them. Because in Mariana's school, evil is never forgotten.

Each page of this story will take you one step closer to the truth, one step closer to the horror that has remained in the shadows for so long. I invite you to delve into this tale with the children, explore the cracks of time and memory, and discover that sometimes terror lies not only in what is seen but in what is heard, in what is felt, and in what cannot be forgotten.

CHAPTER 1: WHISPERS OF THE PAST

Welcome to Mariana's school.

But remember, once you cross the door, there is no turning back.

Mariana's school, an apparently peaceful place, held a dark history. In the same building where children now played and studied, it had once been an orphanage, a place where children lived without families. No one at the school knew much about what had happened there, until one day, Teacher Eduardo from sixth grade decided to tell his students a story that had been buried within the old walls of the place.

It was a rainy afternoon, and all the students in the class—Darío, Layna, Claudia, Ibai, Andrea, Pedro, Samuel, Noa, Carolina, and Mateo—were sitting at their desks while Teacher Eduardo approached the board. The atmosphere was tense; the storm outside made the place feel even darker. Eduardo, with his deep voice, began to speak.

"Many years ago, this school was not what it is today. It was an orphanage, where children who had no family lived. But there was something strange about this place, something that many prefer to forget. I was very young when I first heard this story. One day, when I was still a young teacher here, I was told about a girl who lived in this orphanage, named Anastasia."

The children looked at each other, surprised. The name Anastasia sounded like something straight out of a novel.

"Anastasia was a very special girl," Eduardo continued. "It was said that she had a connection to the other side, something that the other children couldn't understand. There were rumors that she could hear voices in the hallways, whispering secrets. But the strangest thing of all was her gaze. The adults at the orphanage said that when she looked at you, you could see things that no one else could see."

The students leaned forward, captivated, as Eduardo told them how Anastasia disappeared one night without a trace. No one had seen or heard anything. The orphanage, left without answers, closed its doors a few months later. However, the legend of Anastasia remained in the shadows of the place, and over the years, the old orphanage was transformed into the school where they now studied.

"Since her disappearance, some say that Anastasia's soul still haunts the halls of the school," Eduardo said, in a darker tone. "The strange noises at night, the lights that turn off by themselves, the shadows that move for no reason... Many have experienced them, but no one has been able to explain it."

The students, who until that moment had only thought of the story as a simple tale to pass the time, began to look around nervously.

"But... what happened to her?" asked Darío, the most curious of the group.

Eduardo sighed and looked out the window, where the rain was falling heavily.

"No one knows, Darío. Some think that her soul never left. Others say she was searching for something... something that got lost in this place. And maybe... someday, someone will discover the truth."

As the teacher finished speaking, the bell signaling the end of the class rang throughout the school. The children left the classroom with a strange feeling. As they walked down the halls, some stayed behind, staring at the old walls, wondering if Anastasia was still there, watching them from the shadows.

That night, as the sun set and the school fell silent, something strange happened. Claudia, while walking home, swore she heard footsteps behind her, but when she turned around, she saw no one. Carolina noticed how the lights in classroom 3 turned off by themselves, as if someone was playing with the switches. And Mateo, while walking down the hall that led to the old playroom, saw a figure in the doorway, its eyes fixed on him. It couldn't be anyone else, but as he approached, the figure disappeared.

The students couldn't stop thinking about Anastasia's story and wondered if there might be more to it than what the teacher had told them. They decided to investigate on their own.

One afternoon, after classes, Darío, Layna, Claudia, Ibai, Andrea, Pedro, Samuel, Noa, Carolina, and Mateo gathered in the school library. After reviewing old files, they found a torn letter hidden between the pages of a dusty book. It spoke of an "ancient seal" that had to be found to release Anastasia, something that had never been accomplished, as the orphanage closed before the search could be completed.

The letter mentioned a secret room in the school that no one had discovered. Intrigued and with more questions than answers, the ten friends decided to follow the clues, not knowing that in doing so, they would begin to unearth secrets that would change their lives forever.

They would soon discover that the legend of Anastasia was just the tip of the iceberg, and that the mystery of her disappearance was much closer than they had imagined. Mariana's school held secrets far darker than what its walls revealed.

CHAPTER 2: IN THE SHADOW OF MEMORIES

One afternoon, after school, Pedro invited his friends to his house. They decided it was the perfect time to talk more about the mysterious story of Anastasia. Pedro's family lived in an old house near the school, and his grandmother, Mrs Emilia, had always been a source of mysterious tales. The old lady, known for her wisdom and her love for stories from the past, always spoke of bygone times with a distant gaze, as if remembering secrets that others would prefer to forget.

Pedro, a bit nervous, led them to the kitchen, where his grandmother was sitting by the fireplace, knitting a sweater. Upon seeing them enter, Mrs Emilia looked up, offering a smile, although her eyes reflected deep seriousness.

"What brings you here, kids?" she asked with a soft but firm voice, as if she already knew what they were looking for.

Pedro hesitated for a moment, glancing at his friends before speaking.

"Grandma, we're investigating the school. About what happened at the old orphanage. Teacher Eduardo told us something about a girl named Anastasia... Do you know anything about that?"

Mrs Emilia remained silent for a moment, observing them with a piercing gaze, as if evaluating how far they wanted to go. Finally, she placed the sweater on the table and began to speak in a low voice.

"Anastasia... That name always brings dark memories. I was young when the orphanage was still running. I lived not far from it, and my mother, who had worked there, would tell me about many strange things that happened there."

The children leaned in closer to the table, hanging on to every word of Mrs Emilia.

"Anastasia wasn't like the other children. Not just because of her gaze... but something else. My mother told me that people who got too close to her began hearing strange things: whispers, low voices, as if the air itself was filled with secrets. They said Anastasia had the power to see what others couldn't see, that sometimes she spoke to something no one else could see... something from the beyond."

Samuel frowned.

"And what happened to her? Why did she disappear?"

The grandmother sighed, a flicker of sadness in her eyes.

"Anastasia didn't leave... they made her leave," she said, as if those words were hard to say. "My mother told me there was something... something that changed everything. One night, something happened at the orphanage. No one knew exactly what, but that night, when a terrible storm hit the town, the children began behaving strangely. They said Anastasia had been in a locked room, one no one dared to open. That night, she... disappeared."

Layna, with wide eyes, asked, "But how did she disappear? Didn't anyone see her?"

Mrs Emilia nodded slowly.

"No, no one saw her. Some said her room's door was locked, but they heard laughter... a child's laughter, one that wasn't Anastasia's. That laughter echoed throughout the orphanage, but when the adults arrived, she was gone. No one saw her leave. No one ever saw her again. But... since then, it was said that her soul never left the place."

Pedro, hearing this, fell into deep thought. Something in what his grandmother had said resonated with the story he had heard at school. The mention of the laughter and the locked door made him think of something bigger, something deeper than just the disappearance of a girl.

"Grandma... where is that room? Has anyone ever found it?" he asked, with a spark of curiosity.

Mrs Emilia looked at him intently, and her face hardened.

"That room... no one knows where it is. No one has dared to search for it. After Anastasia's disappearance, the orphanage was shut down. Many of those who worked there stopped talking about what happened, as if they feared that speaking about it would condemn them. Some say the room is still there, hidden, waiting to be discovered."

The atmosphere grew heavy with silence. The kids looked at each other, understanding that they weren't just investigating an old legend; they were about to face something much bigger and more dangerous.

Pedro, in a low voice, said, "So, do you think Anastasia is still here? That her spirit is in the school?"

Mrs Emilia slowly rose and moved toward the window. She stared at the stormy sky for a long moment before answering:

"What I believe doesn't matter, children. What matters is what you discover. But I warn you of something: there are things that are better left undisturbed. Because once you start searching, you won't be able to stop. And if you find what you're looking for... you won't be ready for what comes next."

With those words, the kids remained silent, reflecting on what they had just heard. They knew that investigating Anastasia was no longer just simple curiosity. Something more, something dark, was calling them, and perhaps, there would be no turning back.

However, that night, as each of them returned home, they knew that something in the school, in the old orphanage turned school, needed to be uncovered. The story of Anastasia was more alive than ever, and now, somehow, it belonged to them.

The Echo of the School

CHAPTER 3: THE ROCKING CHAIR

That same night, after the conversation with Pedro's grandmother, the ten friends gathered again at the school, determined to investigate on their own. The story of Anastasia had left them with a bitter taste, but it also created a growing need to uncover the truth behind the rumors and mysteries surrounding the place where they spent their days.

Mariana's school was dark and silent, except for the sound of rain tapping against the windows. It was late, and the hallways were empty, with no one left except them. They had planned to meet in front of the main entrance as soon as the clock struck 10 at night. None of them knew exactly what they were hoping to find, but their curiosity had led them here, as though an invisible thread was guiding them.

As they walked down the main hallway, the place felt even quieter than usual. The hallway lights flickered, and a cold draft swept through the empty corridors—something they hadn't noticed during the day. As they moved deeper into the building, a peculiar noise began to resonate, something that sounded like it came from one of the classrooms further away, near the back patio.

Creeeek... creak... creak...

The sound was unmistakable: a rocking chair.

Pedro stopped dead in his tracks, looking at his friends with a mix of surprise and fear.

"Did you hear that?" he whispered, his eyes wide open.

"What is that noise?" Layna asked, feeling a pressure in her chest, as though the air had thickened.

Creeeek... creak... creak...

The sound seemed to be coming from Classroom 3, a room that had always been locked and which students rarely had access to. It was an old classroom, with desks covered in dust, and there were rumors that, in the orphanage's days, the room had been used for "special treatments" or to isolate children who behaved… strangely. Some said it was haunted.

"Let's go check it out," Mateo said, determined, though the expression on his face showed a mixture of fear and fascination.

With hesitant steps, the group made their way toward Classroom 3. The hallway grew darker, the flickering lights barely illuminating the edges of the walls. Each step they took seemed to amplify the sound of the rocking chair. Creeeek... creak... creak... It was as if someone was slowly sitting down and standing up, rocking it ceaselessly.

Finally, they reached the door to Classroom 3. It was

closed, but there was a small crack where a faint light seeped through. No one dared to touch the door immediately. Andrea, the most cautious of them, tried to look through the crack.

"Do you see anything? There's no one inside..." she said softly, though something in her tone didn't convince the others.

Despite the fact that no one seemed to be inside, the sound continued relentlessly. It was as if someone was sitting there, rocking the chair with an unsettling calmness. The sensation that something was watching them began to weigh heavily in the air.

"I don't like this..." Noa whispered, looking around at everyone. "This... isn't right."

Pedro, his heart pounding, gently pushed the door. To his surprise, the door opened with little resistance, as though it had already been slightly ajar, waiting to be opened.

Inside the classroom, the air was dense and cold. The place smelled old, of wet wood, and something forgotten. The desks were covered in dust, and in the center of the room, in the farthest corner, stood an ancient wooden rocking chair, moving slowly, with a constant creaking sound. There was no one in it, but the movement was undeniable.

Creeeek... creak... creak...

Samuel, unable to resist, cautiously approached the rocking chair while the others watched from the door. As he got closer, he noticed something strange on the floor, something that glimmered faintly in the light of his flashlight.

It was a small, old key, covered in dust, but still with engraved details on its metal.

"What's this?" Samuel asked, raising the key in the air.

But at that moment, the rocking chair suddenly stopped.

An absolute silence filled the classroom, and a chill ran down everyone's spines. None of them dared to move.

Suddenly, a soft voice, almost inaudible, was heard in the air. It was a whisper, one that seemed to come from everywhere at once.

"You shouldn't be here..."

It was the voice of a child, but they couldn't tell where it came from. They all looked at each other, fear gripping their hearts.

"It's Anastasia," Claudia whispered, her eyes as wide as saucers. "She's here. She's watching us."

Creeeek... creak... creak... The sound of the rocking chair returned, but this time, it wasn't just a creaking noise. It was the sound of something awakening, something that had been waiting to be released.

The kids, paralyzed by fear, realized that the small key in Samuel's hands wasn't a coincidence. It was the key to unraveling what had been hidden in that classroom, what had been lying dormant for years.

And now, something had begun to awaken.

"We need to leave," Darío said, his voice broken with fear. But before he could take a step back, the door slammed shut, trapping them in the darkness of Classroom 3.

The mystery of Anastasia, the sound of the rocking chair, and the key in their hands had brought them closer to the truth, but also to something much more dangerous.

The Echo of the School

CHAPTER 4: THE NOTE UNDER THE BROKEN TILE

The atmosphere at Mariana's school had changed that night. After the unsettling experience in Classroom 3 and the appearance of the key, the kids weren't sure if they were closer to the truth or if they were simply diving into a mystery from which they couldn't escape. They decided to return the next day, fearful but determined, to continue their investigation. They had a strange feeling, as if something were watching them, guiding them with every step they took.

The next day, during history class, while Teacher Eduardo explained the content about ancient civilizations, something strange happened. Pedro, who had been absentmindedly looking down the hallway, saw something that chilled him to the bone.

Near the main entrance, on the floor of the hallway, was something he didn't remember seeing before: a broken tile, right in the middle of the path. The crack was so perfect that it looked as if someone had broken it on purpose. It wasn't just any crack; it was an odd fracture, as if something heavy had fallen there.

Intrigued, Pedro cautiously approached, followed by the others. The broken tile seemed freshly damaged, as if something or someone had broken it recently. Most of the tiles in this hallway were old, but they were in perfect condition, so this crack seemed out of place.

Suddenly, something caught Carolina's attention. In the small space between the broken ceramic pieces, there was a folded note, as if it had been waiting to be found. Without thinking much, Carolina bent down and picked it up, her hands trembling. The note was made of yellowed, fragile paper, almost disintegrating between her fingers. The writing on it was barely legible, but they managed to make out a few words:

The cycle doesn't end. Find the door, and you will know. The key is not enough. She wants you to do it.

The note had no signature, just those strange words that left a feeling of unease in the air.

— What does this mean? — Andrea asked, staring at the note with a confused expression. — Who wrote it?

Samuel, the most logical of the group, tried to offer an explanation, but he knew that what they were experiencing no longer made sense.

— Someone probably left it here to confuse us. But I can't deny that this... this is getting much stranger.

At that moment, Layna, who had been staring intently at the broken tile, pointed out something that had gone unnoticed: the outline of the crack in the floor. Something was faintly shining beneath it.

— Do you see that? There's something beyond the crack.

Curious and somewhat fearful, the kids began to clear away the dirt and dust that had accumulated under the broken tile. After a few minutes of work, what appeared before them took their breath away. Beneath the tile was a small compartment with a strange object inside. It was a very small wooden box, with a rusty lock on its front.

The box was sealed, but there was something peculiar: it had a small slit, as if it were designed to receive a key. The key Samuel had found in Classroom 3. All eyes turned to him, and a heavy air filled the space.

— Should we... use it? — Claudia asked, her voice trembling.

Pedro nodded, his heart racing. They knew they were about to uncover something important, but they also knew it would bring them even closer to the dark mystery surrounding Mariana's school and its connection to Anastasia.

With trembling hands, Samuel inserted the key into the slit of the box. At first, nothing happened, but when he turned the key, a click echoed in the air. The lid of the box slowly opened, revealing a small object that appeared ancient and mysterious. Inside was a silver medal, with strange symbols engraved on it, some of which the kids couldn't recognize. The medal had an inscription in Latin that read:

Nunc veni, nunc exsisto

("Now I come, now I exist")

It was a disturbing inscription. No one spoke for a moment. They just stared at the medal, wondering if this was part of Anastasia's fate, or if, somehow, they had unleashed something they couldn't control.

The atmosphere grew heavier. The rocking chair, the key, the box... everything seemed to be connected, and what had started as a simple mystery story was now turning into something much larger, much more dangerous.

— I think we've found something we shouldn't have touched, — said Darío, his voice trembling.

But before they could react, the familiar sound of a rocking chair echoed in the distance, this time much closer, as if someone was rocking it again.

Creeeek... creak... creak...

The whisper that accompanied the sound was unmistakable.

— Now, she's coming, — Andrea whispered, fear in her voice, as the medal faintly glimmered in her hands.

CHAPTER 5: THE DARK PRESENCE

The air in the school hallway grew denser, as if something invisible was drawing closer. The silver medal in Samuel's hands glowed faintly, as if it had a life of its own, but the kids didn't dare look at it for too long. The sound of the rocking chair continued to echo in the distance, near Classroom 3, and with each passing moment, it felt closer, more... present.

Pedro, looking at the medal in Samuel's hand, felt a strange compulsion to move.

— There's something else, — he whispered. — I don't know how to explain it, but something is calling us.

With the medal in hand and palpable fear in the air, they crouched once more in front of the broken tile in the hallway. Pedro noticed something that had gone unnoticed until that moment. Beneath the crack in the broken tile, a faint glow was coming from a much deeper gap in the ground. They decided to explore further.

Using one of the old garden shovels they had found in a nearby shed, they began to remove the tiles and dirt. Suddenly, a large stone slab appeared beneath the crack, and as they moved it, a dull sound echoed, as if something ancient and heavy was shifting.

When the slab was completely removed, what they

found took their breath away: a metal hatch leading to a dark and narrow basement.

— This... this was here all along? — Claudia asked, a lump in her throat, staring at the opening.

Samuel, who had been the first to approach the hole, saw that it wasn't just any basement. There was something sinister in the air, something that couldn't be seen at first glance, but was present, like a shadow gliding along the walls. The cold air emanating from the hole chilled their bones, as if time inside that place had come to a standstill.

— I don't know if this is a good idea... — Layna said, her voice trembling, but despite her fears, she couldn't help feeling drawn to the unknown.

Finally, Pedro, feeling the decision weighed on him, stepped forward. With a sigh, he began to descend the rusty iron stairs. The others reluctantly followed. Each step they took made the sound of their footsteps echo through the walls of the tunnel, but what truly unsettled them wasn't the sound of their own steps, but the presence they felt with every breath they took.

The basement was cold and dark. When they finally reached the bottom, they realized it wasn't just a storage room. The space was large, with walls covered in mold and age. In the center, on a stone pedestal, there was a large dark glass urn.

But what caught their attention most was the presence

they felt. Something wasn't right. The feeling of being watched was so strong it was impossible to ignore.

— What is this? — Andrea whispered, looking around as if the shadows were about to consume them. — This... this is wrong.

Suddenly, a deep vibration ran through the ground, as if the place was about to open. The shadows seemed to move, and a soft, almost imperceptible laugh floated in the air, freezing their blood.

You shouldn't have come...

The voice didn't come from anywhere, but seemed to resonate in their heads. It was as if it were echoing in the very space around them, in the heavy air that surrounded them.

Pedro, with his heart racing, stepped forward toward the urn. He couldn't shake the feeling that something inside it was calling to him. It was as if the object were alive, and the sensation of power and darkness grew stronger with each passing second.

When Pedro touched the glass, an invisible force pushed him back, knocking him away with an unexpected violence. The urn began to vibrate and glow with a dark, almost liquid light. And then, as if everything that had happened until that moment had only been the prelude to something greater, the darkness began to materialize.

From the depths of the urn, a shadowy figure emerged, distorted and blurry, but clearly human. It had no face, but there was something about it that made them recognize it instantly.

It was Anastasia.

Or at least, what remained of her. Her body floated like an ethereal silhouette, her presence filling the entire basement with a cold and malignant energy. Her eyes, empty and dark, glowed with an intensity that froze their hearts.

The laughter returned, louder now, and the ground trembled beneath their feet.

— You shouldn't have touched the medal! — said a voice, now clear, from the figure of Anastasia, speaking through her spectral form. — Now everything will be unleashed!

At that moment, the shadows of the basement began to move violently, crawling along the walls and ceiling. The dark presence that had been stalking them was taking shape. Something much older and more dangerous than Anastasia herself had been released with her awakening. A being that fed on fear, on lost souls, and that had been waiting for the right moment to claim dominion over everything forgotten in this ancient orphanage turned school.

Pedro, his heart in his throat, watched as the figure of Anastasia slowly faded, leaving behind a reddish light and a whisper that pierced their bones:

— The cycle doesn't end... now I will possess you...

The group, paralyzed by fear and horror, began to feel the darkness closing in around them. The basement was no longer just a hidden place, but a portal, a space where the slumbering evil had begun to awaken. And now, not only they, but everyone at the school, was in danger.

And the worst part was, there was no turning back.

The Echo of the School

CHAPTER 6: THE LOST SHOES

The atmosphere at Mariana's school was growing heavier. After the terrifying revelation in the basement and the awakening of the dark presence that dwelled in the shadows, the group of friends could not stop feeling watched. The medallion, the urn, and the spectral figure of Anastasia haunted their thoughts as they tried to find a way to stop what had been set in motion. However, what happened next left them utterly stunned.

It was a gray and cloudy day, typical of the colder winter months. The kids were gathered in the classroom, sitting at their desks, trying to continue with their studies, although none of them could really concentrate. Fear and uncertainty surrounded them like a thick fog, and they could still feel the echoes of the dark presence they had unleashed.

Suddenly, a scream broke the silence.

— Darío! —shouted Claudia.

Everyone quickly looked toward the back of the room, where Darío, the calmest and most composed of them all, had been sitting at his desk, focused on his books. But now... he was gone. His chair was empty.

Panic began to flood the room. No one had seen him leave, and no one had heard any noise indicating that he had gotten up. The classroom door was closed, and the windows were shut as well. How had he disappeared so suddenly?

— Where is Darío? —asked Layna, her voice trembling.

They all quickly stood up, searching every corner of the room, calling his name, but Darío was nowhere to be found. The room seemed even emptier than usual, and an oppressive feeling began to fill the air.

Pedro, with adrenaline coursing through his veins, was the first to run out into the hallway. He hurried down the hall, opening the doors of nearby classrooms, but Darío was nowhere to be found.

— Darío, where are you?! —yelled Pedro, desperate. But only the echo of his own voice responded.

Finally, as he reached the entrance of the school, something caught his attention. In the threshold of the main door, on the cold, wet floor, were a pair of shoes.

His shoes.

It was so strange that Pedro couldn't understand what he was seeing. There was no trace of Darío, but there, in front of him, were his sneakers, perfectly aligned on the floor, as if he had dropped them while walking. There were no footprints, no clues as to where he had gone. The shoes weren't disheveled or dirty; they were simply there, as if someone had decided to leave them behind and walk away without another thought.

— These are his shoes! —Pedro said, a lump in his throat. — But where is he?

The others came running behind him, and when they saw the shoes, a chill ran down their spines. They couldn't understand what had happened. How could someone disappear, leaving only their shoes behind?

Carolina, the most sensitive of the group, started hyperventilating.

— This... this isn't right. It's like in ghost stories... when someone disappears but leaves something behind, like a sign... —she said, her voice trembling.

Andrea looked around, searching for any logical explanation, but there was none.

— We can't stay here! We have to do something... Darío is gone! —said Samuel, starting to panic.

The group of friends stared at the shoes with growing horror, wondering what this strange disappearance meant. They had faced inexplicable horrors in the past weeks, but this was something completely different. It was as if Darío had been swallowed by the very air itself, leaving only his shoes as traces of his existence.

As the group debated between fear and confusion, a distant, distorted laugh reached their ears, as if someone was enjoying the chaos they had just unleashed. Anastasia's laugh resonated in their minds, like a whisper that froze their blood.

The cycle is complete, said the voice in their heads, now clearer, stronger.

With their hearts in their throats, Pedro picked up the shoes, but at that moment, something changed in the air. The feeling of being watched intensified, as if the entire school had transformed into a massive tunnel of shadows closing in around them.

— It's trapping us... —murmured Claudia, her eyes wide open.

The cycle hasn't ended... it's just beginning, whispered the same voice, this time from within the room, where Darío had been sitting just moments ago.

The group then understood that Darío's disappearance wasn't an accident. The dark presence that had been released in the basement, the medallion, Anastasia's whisper—everything seemed connected. And now, one of them was gone, leaving behind a strange clue: his shoes.

But... why? What did this mean? Was it a warning? Or something much more sinister?

Meanwhile, the sound of the rocking chair began to creak again, louder than ever, this time not from classroom 3, but from somewhere much closer, as if it were right behind them.

Creeeeek... creak... creak...

And everything at Mariana's school seemed to indicate that Darío, far from leaving, had been claimed by something much darker and older. And they, now, were closer than ever to the mystery that had been waiting patiently to emerge into the light.

The Echo of the School

CHAPTER 7: THE SUSPICION

Panic had fully settled into Mariana's school. Darío's disappearance had left the group of students trembling, without answers, only the unsettling image of his shoes left behind at the threshold of the main door. No one understood how someone could vanish like that, let alone why only their shoes remained, as if their presence had vanished into thin air.

However, the worst was yet to come.

It was late afternoon when the kids were gathered in the library, trying to find any clues in the old history books of the school, searching for something that might help them understand what was happening. Fear still hung over them, and the echo of Anastasia's laughter seemed to follow them through every corner of the school. No one wanted to be alone, but they knew they had to find a solution.

That's when something else happened.

Another student disappeared.

This time it was Ibai. No one saw him leave, nor did they hear the sound of his chair moving or the door opening. He simply wasn't there. The kids began calling his name, walking through the hallways, searching the school corridors, but Ibai didn't respond.

Fear took hold of them when they saw, once again, a pair of shoes.

Ibai's shoes.

They were right in front of the door to classroom 3, perfectly aligned, as if someone had deliberately placed them there. No one could believe it. Darío's disappearance, now Ibai's. And the strangest thing of all—these shoes kept appearing, as if the place were marked by the disappearance of each of their classmates.

— This can't be a coincidence, murmured Carolina, staring at the shoes in horror. Something is happening here. Something is taking them.

Eduardo, the sixth-grade teacher, appeared in the hallway at that moment, his face pale and serious, as if he weren't surprised by the situation. He had been giving lessons, but his eyes didn't show the same concern as the kids. He seemed... distant, somewhat disconnected, as if he already knew more than he let on.

— What happened here? —Eduardo asked, his voice deep, looking at Ibai's shoes without showing any sign of surprise.

The teacher's reaction seemed strange to them. Why wasn't he more concerned? Why didn't he seem scared like they did? The kids exchanged looks, beginning to suspect something. There was something wrong with

Eduardo. His mysterious behavior made them feel like there was something he wasn't telling them. What if he knew more than he was letting on?

Pedro, with his heart racing, was the first to speak.

— Teacher... where were you when Darío disappeared? —he asked, his gaze fixed on Eduardo.

Eduardo blinked and then responded, his tone cold and calculated.

— I... was in my office. I have nothing to do with this, guys. I know this is terrifying, but we need to stay calm.

The kids weren't convinced. There was something in his voice that didn't add up, something in his eyes that told them he wasn't telling them the whole truth. As he looked at them, his eyes reflected no fear or concern, but... something darker. Confusion, but also a kind of resignation.

Claudia, with a look of distrust, stepped forward.

— Why aren't you surprised, Teacher? Two students have disappeared... and you seem so... calm?

Eduardo looked at Claudia with an expressionless face, as if he had already anticipated the question. Then, without taking his eyes off them, he said:

— What's happening isn't something we can control. You already knew, didn't you? The cycle... the cycle doesn't end.

Those words were enough for all the kids to look at each other, paralyzed by growing fear. Eduardo seemed to know more than he was saying. What did he mean by the cycle? What did he know about Darío's disappearance and now about Ibai's?

— What cycle? —asked Andrea, her voice trembling, unable to hide the fear in her eyes.

Eduardo sighed deeply, as if he were tired of hiding the truth.

— Anastasia... it wasn't an accident. What happened in the orphanage... what happened to her... didn't end. The ones who came after, the ones who stayed here... they couldn't just leave. They're trapped in this place, in a cycle... a cycle that must be completed.

Each word Eduardo spoke weighed heavily in the air. No one fully understood what he meant, but the terror that gripped them was immediate. What cycle? And why did Eduardo seem to know so much about all of this?

Suddenly, the kids understood that it wasn't just about inexplicable disappearances anymore. They were now dealing with something much bigger, and their teacher might be linked to it in some way, perhaps even as part of the cycle he mentioned.

The tension was palpable, and the fear multiplied with every word Eduardo spoke. But before they could ask him more questions, Eduardo raised a hand, signaling for silence.

— It doesn't matter what you do. They will come for all of you. And you are next.

The atmosphere in the room grew heavy. The kids, now with terror evident in their eyes, looked at Eduardo with a mix of disbelief and horror. Darío's disappearance, now Ibai's, and now the teacher's words confirmed what they all feared: something much bigger and darker was in motion, and Eduardo didn't just seem to know about it—he was somehow involved.

— It's trapping all of us —murmured Samuel, his eyes filled with terror.

At that moment, the rocking chair began to creak again, this time much louder than before, as if it were getting closer, as if the evil was about to claim them one by one. The sound of the rocking chair was the signal that the cycle was nearing completion, and now all of them were part of it.

— There's no escape now —whispered Eduardo, his voice darker than before.

And the echo of those words resonated in their minds as they felt the dark presence approaching, ever closer, claiming what was its own.

The Echo of the School

CHAPTER 8: A NEW STUDENT

The tension in Mariana's school was palpable. After the disappearances of Darío and Ibai, uncertainty and fear had taken hold of everyone. The strange presence that had awakened in the basement, the silver medal, and Eduardo's warnings had left them teetering on the edge of an abyss. No one knew for sure what was happening, but one thing was clear: something dark loomed over them, and the disappearances weren't going to stop.

It was amidst this growing darkness that, unexpectedly, a new student arrived at the school. His name was Rayan, and although no one was expecting him, his arrival was not as surprising as the fact that he came at such a tense moment, when the school seemed to be shrouded in an invisible shadow.

Rayan was unlike the others. Although he was only 12 years old, his gaze revealed a maturity that was unusual for a boy his age. He was a quiet, calm child, with dark hair and eyes that always seemed to be searching for something, as if he were constantly alert. His uniform was perfectly pressed, but there was something in his behavior that didn't quite fit, as if he were aware that he didn't fully belong to this place.

When Rayan walked through the school's front door, all eyes turned to him. The students, nervous and fearful, couldn't help but watch him, but Rayan seemed unfazed by their stares. In fact, it almost seemed as though he already knew what was happening, as if he was prepared for what was to come.

On his first day, Teacher Eduardo introduced him to the class.

— This is Rayan, said Eduardo, his voice void of emotion. A new student. Treat him well.

The kids looked at him with suspicion, especially after what had happened with Darío and Ibai. No one dared to talk to him much, but Rayan didn't seem bothered. Instead of being shy or confused, he simply nodded and sat down calmly. His presence, though silent, seemed to carry an air of mystery that only fueled the suspicions of others.

As the classes continued, Pedro, Claudia, Carolina, and the others couldn't help but watch Rayan. There was something about him that didn't fit, but they didn't know what it was.

The rest of the students also felt a strange unease seeing him, though no one dared to speak to him much. All they knew was that, in an atmosphere so thick with tension, Rayan's arrival seemed like a forewarning of something even darker.

But the strange events began that very afternoon. Rayan had been sitting at his desk, reading a book, when a strange sound began to fill the air. It was like a murmur, something low, almost inaudible. The kids thought it came from the classroom, but they couldn't pinpoint where it was coming from. The feeling of unease grew, and everyone, without exception, felt a strange and disturbing presence.

Suddenly, the classroom lights began to flicker, and everyone looked at each other, terrified. Something was happening, something out of their control.

Pedro, who had been watching Rayan with growing distrust, noticed something odd: the boy didn't flinch. He was so calm that it seemed as if he wasn't affected by the rising anxiety in the air. This made Pedro feel even more uneasy.

It was then that Rayan slowly lifted his head, looked around the room at everyone, and with an unsettling calm, said:

— I know what's going on here. And I know there's no turning back.

The room fell into a deathly silence. No one dared to speak, and they all stared at Rayan, as if waiting for him to explain what he had just said.

— I know what's going on... I know what's coming, he repeated, with a calmness so terrifying that it sent chills down the spine of each student present.

How could he know? How could Rayan, a new boy, know something that they themselves didn't fully understand?

Claudia, unable to hold herself back, stepped forward and asked:

— What are you talking about? How do you know... how do you know what's happening here?

Rayan smiled slightly, but it wasn't a warm or friendly smile. It was an odd smile, as if he was privy to a dark secret that the others couldn't even begin to imagine.

— Because I'm not like you. And this place... it's not what it seems.

The students exchanged looks, confused and terrified, but there was no time for more questions. Just then, the sound of the rocking chair began to creak again, louder than ever. This time, it seemed to be coming directly from the basement, the closed room that had already tormented them before.

Rayan slowly stood up from his seat, and with a serious expression, he began walking toward the classroom door. The others watched him, not daring to stop him, but they knew something important was about to happen.

— It's time for everyone to know the truth, said Rayan, as if those words were a forewarning of something terrible. And with that statement, he began to walk toward the hallway, heading toward the basement.

The group of friends, horrified but also with a strange sense that Rayan knew something they didn't, decided to follow him. There was no turning back. The darkness that had been stalking them had come to claim what it was owed. And now, Rayan could be the key to understanding what was happening in Mariana's school.

But what secrets was he really hiding? Why did he seem so calm while everything around him was falling apart? The question lingered in everyone's mind, but they knew it was time to face the truth, no matter how terrifying it might be.

The cycle was about to be completed.

The Echo of the School

CHAPTER 9: THE BLACK CAT

When the kids decided to follow Rayan, a strange and heavy atmosphere took over the entire school. As they neared the basement, the tension grew. The mysterious new student, with his distant gaze and unsettling words, led them toward an uncertain fate. No one knew what they would find in that dark and desolate place, but something in their hearts told them they couldn't stop now. The truth was about to be revealed.

The hallway to the basement was dark, and although the lights flickered intermittently, the kids could see the steep stairs leading down into the unknown. The sound of footsteps echoed on the wood, and each of the kids felt as if the darkness was closing in around them, almost as if the school itself were alive, watching them.

Rayan walked in front, unperturbed, as if he were familiar with every corner of the place. The others followed, nervous but determined. The cycle, as he had said, was about to be completed, and the sense that something terrible was about to unfold intensified with each step.

Suddenly, when they reached the bottom of the stairs, something strange happened. A presence made them stop dead in their tracks.

A black cat, with glowing eyes, appeared in the dim

light of the hallway that stretched before them. The feline stood at the threshold of the door leading to the basement. Its fur was as dark as the night itself, and its eyes reflected a faint green light, as if they contained ancient secrets. The creature stared at them fixedly, unmoving, as if waiting for them to do something.

— A cat... —murmured Carolina, feeling uncomfortable—. What is it doing here?

Rayan didn't seem surprised to see the cat. In fact, he looked almost expectant, as if he had been waiting for it.

— This cat —said Rayan— is a guide. Do not fear it. It will show you the way.

The kids exchanged puzzled glances. A cat as a guide? What did Rayan mean by that? The air grew even heavier. The cat, with its glowing eyes in the dark, watched them in silence, but somehow, they felt that the feline was connected to everything that had been happening at the school.

— This cat is not ordinary. It is a manifestation of the place, of what happened here —explained Rayan, slowly crouching down—. Of what has always been lurking, and what is now about to awaken.

Rayan seemed to know too much.

The cat, however, did not move. It simply remained there, unmoving, its gaze fixed on the kids. But then, almost imperceptibly, it turned and ventured into the darkness of the hallway, inviting them to follow. The basement door was close, and the cat seemed to be pointing the way.

The fear grew even more. If they had already been afraid of what they might find below, now they knew this cat was more than just an animal. Was it a sign of the dark presence that haunted the school? Was it a guide to something even darker?

Despite the growing sense of danger, the kids, driven by the need to understand what was happening, decided to follow the cat. Rayan, as if he were the leader of the expedition, walked confidently behind the feline.

The cat, seeing they were following, began to move faster, crossing the shadows of the house with supernatural grace, guiding them toward a door at the end of the hallway. The basement door. When they reached the entrance, the cat stopped, staring inside, as if waiting for someone to take the first step.

Suddenly, the feeling of being watched grew even more. The atmosphere became dense, filled with a dark energy that invaded them. The kids felt that something was waiting down there, something ancient and evil, as if the basement were the center of everything that had been happening. And now, with the appearance of the black cat, the cycle was drawing near its end.

Rayan, with unwavering calm, looked at the kids and

said:

— This is just the beginning. What we find down there will reveal everything you need to know... and everything you must fear.

The cat gave one last look at the group, as if granting its blessing for them to continue, and then crossed the door, disappearing into the darkness of the basement.

The door creaked open, and the group, hearts in their throats, took the first step into the darkness. There was no turning back.

The black cat had been only the first of many omens, and what awaited them down in the basement... was something that would change their lives forever.

CHAPTER 10: THE GRANDFATHER

As the kids crossed the door into the basement, the air grew colder and denser. The darkness seemed to swallow them whole, and the sound of their own footsteps echoed on the walls like a distant hum. They all followed Rayan, who moved forward fearlessly, as though he already knew every corner of the place. The black cat, whose presence had been so unsettling, seemed to have vanished into the blackness of the hallway, but something inside them told them it was nearby, watching them.

As they descended the stairs, the atmosphere grew more unsettling with each step. The cycle, as Rayan had said, was close to being completed, and a sense of inevitable fate filled the air. When they reached the bottom of the stairs, a faint light came from an old lamp flickering weakly in the corner of the room. The basement was filled with old furniture covered in white sheets, dusty boxes, and objects that seemed to have been there for decades.

The group stopped as they reached the center of the basement. The silence was absolute, and a sense of dark presence surrounded them. It was then that Rayan, with his soft but grave voice, broke the silence.

— This place holds more secrets than you can imagine. And there's something I must tell you... something about my grandfather, which is directly related to everything that has been happening here.

The kids exchanged surprised glances but decided to listen. If Rayan knew something about what was going on, they needed to hear it. Rayan began to walk slowly through the shadows of the basement, as though he were recalling what he was about to say.

— My grandfather... he wasn't an ordinary man, he began, his voice now taking on a darker tone. He knew the past of this place much better than anyone who's been here. I used to visit him at his house, and for years he told me stories about the old orphanage that stood here before the school was built.

The silence in the basement heightened the tension in the air. The kids, hearts racing, awaited more details. What did Rayan's grandfather know about the orphanage?

— My grandfather worked here when he was young, at the orphanage, Rayan continued. He was one of the few who still dared to enter. The orphanage was full of mysteries, and he would always talk to me about a woman named Anastasia. No one knew much about her, but they said she was different. Rumors circulated that she was connected to what happened here, something beyond what the adults were willing to admit.

Claudia, unable to contain her curiosity, interrupted.

— Anastasia? Who was she? What happened to her?

Rayan looked at them, and with a somber expression, he answered:

— Anastasia wasn't an ordinary orphan. She came to the orphanage under strange circumstances. My grandfather told me that Anastasia had a power, something inexplicable that others didn't understand. Some said she could see things that others couldn't, as if she were connected to a dark energy that emanated from the orphanage walls. Sometimes, they would hear strange laughter or footsteps that didn't belong to anyone. But the most unsettling thing was what happened to her when she disappeared.

The group of kids leaned in closer, feeling that Rayan's story was about to reveal something crucial.

— My grandfather told me that Anastasia disappeared one night without a trace. No one saw her leave, and no one heard anything. But the strangest part was that after her disappearance, strange things began happening at the orphanage. Some said the place was cursed, that Anastasia's spirit hadn't left, that something of her remained trapped in those walls.

The kids, now completely captivated by the story, felt a chill run down their spines. The connection between Anastasia and the unease in the school was beginning to make more sense, but there was still something that didn't fit.

— My grandfather explained to me that Anastasia's power, and what she left behind, stayed in the place.

When the orphanage was closed and the school was built in its place, some of the orphanage's former employees tried to seal the curse, but they were unsuccessful. In fact, he told me that every generation, those who lived or studied here, were part of a cycle, one that began when the darkness awoke in the basement.

Rayan paused, looking at the group with intensity. He knew his words were making everything more real, and everyone was about to understand what was coming.

— My grandfather also warned me about the black cat. He wasn't just an animal, but a guardian. He's always been here, watching, waiting for the right moment to help. But he also told me that those who crossed the threshold of the basement... would never be the same again.

The kids looked at each other, terrified, as Rayan's words sank into their minds. Was the black cat really a guardian? And what would happen to them if they continued descending into this abyss with no return?

— What we don't understand, Rayan continued, is that Anastasia never left. Her spirit is still here, trapped in this cycle, and now it's looking for those who will complete it. We are the chosen ones, just like the orphans, the orphanage workers... all part of a plan that began long ago.

The silence in the basement became overwhelming.

Suddenly, everything seemed clearer and yet more terrifying. The cycle Rayan had spoken of, the dark presence, the black cat, Anastasia… it all seemed interconnected, and now they were involved in something far greater than they had imagined.

Rayan looked at the kids one last time.

— If we choose to continue, it will be our decision. But you must know that what's down here is not just waiting to be set free. It's searching for something, and now that we're here, the cycle is about to be completed.

With those words, Rayan walked toward the dark entrance of the basement, the weight of his grandfather's story heavy on his shoulders. The group of kids followed him, but they knew there would be no turning back. They were about to face the truth, no matter how terrifying it might be.

The black cat, from some corner in the darkness, watched them. And they, still unaware, were about to release what had been waiting for generations.

The Echo of the School

CHAPTER 11: BETRAYAL

The atmosphere in the basement grew heavier with every step they took. The story Rayan had told them about his grandfather and the mysterious cycle of darkness surrounding Mariana's school had left them with a deep sense of unease. As they moved deeper into the basement, surrounded by dusty furniture and elongated shadows, an odd presence seemed to draw nearer.

Suddenly, a noise broke the silence. A creaking sound came from one of the basement walls, as if something was moving behind the stone. The group stopped, looking in every direction. They could all feel something watching them, but they didn't know what it was or where it was coming from.

It was at that moment that a figure appeared in the dim light.

It was Eduardo, the sixth-grade teacher. The group immediately recognized him, but his unexpected appearance in the basement caused a great deal of discomfort. What was he doing down here?

Eduardo didn't seem surprised to see them. In fact, he seemed almost expectant. His face, usually friendly and calm, was now marked by a serious expression, as if everything happening was part of a plan he already knew all too well.

— Well, it seems you're not scared. That's good, said Eduardo, his voice low and calm, as if he had already prepared for the encounter. Those who are down here can't turn back. There's no point in continuing, but... I suppose you've already made your decision.

The kids exchanged wary glances, a growing sense of distrust bubbling within them. They had been suspicious of Rayan, but now it was Eduardo who was arousing an even stronger feeling of unease.

— Teacher, what's going on here? Claudia asked, her voice trembling but determined. Why are you here? Did you know all of this from the beginning?

Eduardo didn't answer right away. Instead, he took a step toward them, his gaze fixed on the kids as if he were evaluating each one. Eduardo's eyes were glowing strangely, more intense than usual, and no one missed that detail.

— Do you know what's really happening here? he asked, with a smile that didn't reach his eyes. Did you know since you found the medallion? Since the basement began to open again, the cycle began. Nothing will stop it now.

The group of students exchanged glances of suspicion. Something in his words didn't fit. Eduardo didn't seem surprised, not even worried. It seemed as though all of this was part of something he already knew, a game they were unwittingly caught in.

— What do you mean by that, Eduardo? Pedro asked, looking at the teacher with a mixture of fear and confusion. Are you part of this? Part of what happened in the orphanage? Of what happened with Anastasia?

Eduardo finally let out a faint laugh, a laugh that sounded almost empty, without joy, as though something dark were hidden behind it.

— What happened with Anastasia… is only a small part of the story. The real story is much bigger. And if you've made it this far, it means there's no turning back. Like I said, the cycle must be completed.

The group of kids was growing more and more confused. They were starting to wonder if Eduardo was involved in something much darker than they had ever imagined. What did he mean by the cycle? Why was he speaking about the history so distantly, as if it was something he had planned all along?

Suddenly, the atmosphere in the basement grew even denser. The black cat appeared again, its eyes glowing in the dark as it walked toward Eduardo, as if it recognized him or, somehow, had been waiting for him. Was he part of the cycle? Had Eduardo been manipulating everything from the beginning?

— The cat? Noa asked, her voice barely a whisper. Is he the one who follows you, teacher?

Eduardo nodded slowly, never taking his eyes off the cat. His eyes narrowed, and a dark expression crossed his face.

— The black cat has been here long before any of you. He's part of all this. A guardian, as I said. And now, his mission is almost complete.

Eduardo's words echoed what Rayan had said earlier. The cycle was nearing completion, and now they were at the center of it all, unaware of how much their lives had been manipulated to bring them to this point.

The group was starting to doubt Eduardo. Everything seemed to indicate that he wasn't here by accident. His calmness, his knowledge of what was going on, and the strange connection with the black cat made them suspect more and more.

— We can't trust you, can we, teacher? Carolina said, not taking her eyes off him. You told us there was something in the basement, but what you didn't tell us is that you knew everything about Anastasia and the cycle. Isn't that true?

Eduardo didn't answer immediately, but his smile widened.

— Trust me? Is that what you want? I'm not the enemy here, but I must be honest with you. The cycle won't stop. And if you want to survive, you'll have to make decisions you can't even imagine.

The tension in the air grew thick. The kids looked at Eduardo with a mix of fear, distrust, and anger.

Something didn't add up in his words. He knew too much, was too calm, as if all of this was part of a much bigger plan, one in which they were nothing more than pieces of a puzzle he had already assembled.

Before they could say anything else, Eduardo took a step back, as if concluding the encounter.

— Just remember one thing, he said in a cold voice. Nothing can stop what was unleashed here. You are part of this story, and no matter how hard you try, the darkness will always find a way to return.

With those words, Eduardo turned and disappeared into the shadows of the basement. The black cat, just like him, vanished into the darkness, as if they had never been there. The cycle was about to be completed. And now, more than ever, the kids knew they couldn't trust Eduardo. He wasn't just the sixth-grade teacher. He was part of something much larger and darker, something that had been brewing for generations. And now, they were part of that sinister plan that seemed to have no end.

CHAPTER 12: THE LETTER

The atmosphere in the basement remained heavy, filled with tension and mystery. After Eduardo's unsettling appearance, the group stood still, processing everything they had just learned. Something didn't add up. Eduardo had been part of it all from the start, but now the mystery of the disappearances of their friends had grown even more urgent. What had happened to Darío and Ibai? The question weighed on them like an unrelenting shadow.

It was then that Andrea let out a stifled scream, startled by something she had found on an old table in a dark corner of the basement. With trembling hands, she lifted a yellowed letter, carefully folded, as if it had been waiting to be discovered. The letter appeared ancient, and the words written in black ink seemed almost to fade with time.

— Look! It's a letter! Andrea exclaimed, rushing to the others.

With the flickering light of their lamp illuminating the paper, they all gathered quickly to read. The words were clear, but the sentences were cryptic, almost as if they were specifically meant for them.

The letter read as follows:

If you have made it this far, then the cycle has begun.

There is no turning back. Those who have disappeared are trapped in the same fate as you. But there is still hope. Not everything is lost.

The basement holds the key. Not just the place where the secrets were sealed, but also the way to release them. You will find what you seek in the most unexpected place: in the corner that hides in plain sight. Look beneath the old typewriter. There lies what you need to rescue those who are gone.

Time is running out. The cycle will soon be complete. The spirits do not forgive. Only those with the courage to challenge the inevitable will be able to save others. Do not let the cycle consume you all.

With this final message, I leave you hope, but also a warning. If you do not act, you will all become part of what is to come.

The group read in silence, each word resonating deeply within their hearts. The letter seemed to have been written specifically for them, as if someone—perhaps Anastasia—had foreseen their arrival in the basement and wanted to guide them. But there was something in those words that disturbed them even more: the warning that the cycle must be completed.

— What does all this mean? Samuel murmured, not taking his eyes off the letter. What is this 'old typewriter' they're talking about? What are they asking us to do?

They all looked around, searching for any clues. The basement was filled with old objects, furniture covered in white sheets, boxes, and various items in disarray. But what caught everyone's attention was an old typewriter, covered in dust, sitting on a table in the darkest corner of the room. They hadn't noticed it before, but now it stood out, as if it had been waiting for them.

— There it is! Noa shouted, pointing toward the typewriter. It's what the letter says!

The group quickly moved toward the typewriter, and when they lifted it, they found something hidden beneath it on the floor. A small metal box. The sound of the box opening was like a whisper in the dark, a whisper that made everyone pause for a moment, afraid of what they might find inside.

Inside the box was a small rolled-up piece of paper, tied with a red ribbon. Unrolling it, they found what appeared to be a hand-drawn map, with clear instructions on how to find their missing friends. The map showed an undiscovered part of the school, a section of hallways and rooms they had never seen, as if the whole building was built over hidden layers.

— This... this is a map of the school, Carolina said, her eyes wide in shock. But... it's as if the school has secrets no one has told us. Something beneath everything we know.

On the side of the map were a series of strange symbols they didn't recognize, but they seemed to be related to the trapped spirits, almost as if indicating a path toward the lost souls. There was also a note written in urgent handwriting:

To rescue the missing, you must enter the place where time stopped. Where the voices of the orphans still whisper. There you will find what you seek, but you will also discover what the cycle demands.

The group looked at each other in silence, processing the information. It was becoming clearer that the basement and everything connected to the abandoned orphanage were not just legends or superstitions. It was real. And now, with the map in their hands, they knew there was a hidden path, one that could lead them to the places where their missing friends were.

But they also knew this wouldn't be easy. The cycle was nearly complete, and the shadows of the past could no longer stay hidden.

— So... are we ready to follow this map? Mateo asked, looking at the others.

They all nodded silently, their hearts racing. There was something in the letter and the map that told them they couldn't turn back now. The disappearance of their friends was no accident. Everything was tied to the dark mystery of this place, and only by uncovering what had happened in the past could they stop the cycle.

With the letter in hand, the map, and the determination to rescue their friends, the group of kids prepared to face the unknown. The next step would be crucial, and they knew their lives depended on what they would discover in the school's hidden hallways, where time seemed to have stopped and the souls of the lost continued to whisper in the dark.

The true test was about to begin.

The Echo of the School

CHAPTER 13: THE OWL

The group stood in silence, staring at the map with a mixture of determination and fear. They knew that the next step they took would bring them closer to the truth, but it would also lead them into unknown danger. No one wanted to speak first, as the tension was palpable. Each of them was lost in their thoughts, weighing the possible consequences of what they were about to do.

It was then that, in the dim light of the basement, they heard the soft flutter of wings. Everyone turned at once, startled by the sound that seemed to come out of nowhere. In the darkest corner, near the door they had entered, appeared an owl.

At first, they thought it was just an ordinary animal that had wandered into the basement, but they quickly realized that something about the bird was unusual. The owl was a dark gray color, with enormous eyes that reflected the light from their lantern with an almost supernatural glow. Its feathers seemed to shimmer with a faint radiance, and its wings moved with mysterious grace, as if it were floating more than flying.

The owl landed on a nearby table, staring at them intently, as though waiting for them to react. No one dared to take a step, but they all felt that the bird's presence was no accident.

Rayan, the new student, was the first to speak, his voice barely a whisper.

— This isn't normal. In my grandfather's culture, owls are guides. They're like messengers between the world of the living and the dead.

The rest of the group exchanged glances, sensing that the mystery was deepening. The owl, as if understanding their thoughts, let out a soft hoot, almost as if it were trying to get their attention. With a tilt of its head, the owl turned toward the opposite side of the basement, as if indicating for them to follow.

Andrea didn't hesitate. Without another thought, she stepped toward the owl, which fixed its bright eyes on her before taking flight toward the hallway. The group, now determined to follow, began moving after it.

The owl flew along the wall, its wings beating softly as it glided through the darkness. With each movement, it seemed as though the path was illuminated in some way, as if an invisible light was following the bird. The group walked behind it, feeling as though they were being guided by something larger than themselves. The atmosphere in the basement seemed to shift; the walls, once cold and dark, now appeared to be filled with invisible presences, watching them.

The owl led them to a secret passage they had never seen before, a hidden entryway at the back of the basement. They passed through an almost invisible door, and on the other side, they found a small room filled with strange symbols on the walls and floor. The owl landed on a table in the center, stopping its movement, as if waiting for the group to understand something.

— What does this mean? Carolina asked, looking around the room.

In the center of the table sat an ancient wooden box, with the same strange symbols they had seen on the map. The owl stared at them, as if urging them to open the box.

Rayan, sensing that everything had a purpose, stepped forward and, with trembling hands, opened the box. Inside, he found an old key, worn but with a peculiar glow, as if it still held some power.

— This... this must be important, Rayan said, looking at the others. This key... it probably opens a door or leads to another hidden part of the school. Something that's been concealed.

Mateo quickly approached, his mind racing.

— Do you think it will take us to where our friends are? To that hidden room on the map?

The owl, as though it had understood Mateo's words, hooted again, this time more urgently. It looked toward the wall, its bright eyes pointing the way, then spread its wings as if it were ready to fly once more.

— There must be something else here. Maybe the door is close, Claudia said, not taking her eyes off the owl.

The owl began to fly again, guiding them toward a hidden door in the wall. As they neared it, the group noticed that Rayan's key fit perfectly into the lock. The sound of the lock turning echoed down the hallway, as if something ancient had been unlocked, and the door slowly creaked open, revealing what appeared to be a secret vault.

Inside the room were a series of old books, mirrors covered with cloth, and a palpable sense of supernatural presence that was almost overwhelming. The owl flew in and perched on a shelf, watching them as if telling them that what they were searching for was here.

Without hesitation, the group began to sift through the books and objects, feeling that they were closer than ever to solving the mystery of the disappearances and the dark cycle that had begun at the school. Each of them felt the urgency to act quickly before it was too late.

But the owl did not abandon them. Like a spiritual guide, it continued to fly around the room, always a step ahead, showing them the way. The group no longer had any doubts: the owl was not just an ordinary animal. It was a guide, sent to help them break the cycle and rescue their friends.

— What do we do now? Andrea asked, looking at the owl, waiting for a sign.

Once again, the owl fixed its gaze on them and let out a soft hoot, as if telling them that their journey was not yet finished. But this time, the group was no longer afraid. They knew that the owl was guiding them to the answer. The cycle was about to be broken, and all that was left to do was move forward, facing the unknown and the dark past that connected them all.

The Echo of the School

CHAPTER 14: THE ENCOUNTER

The group, guided by the owl, moved down the hidden corridor, their hearts pounding with each step. Every move brought them closer to the mystery, and the feeling that they were on the right path grew stronger. The presence of the owl, which sometimes perched on nearby shelves or tables, remained reassuring, as if they were under the protection of something ancient and wise. Every time they looked at it, its eyes glowed with an inhuman intensity, as if it could see beyond the visible.

Finally, they reached a small hallway at the back of the basement. The owl flew toward a rusted iron door that seemed weathered by time. The door was locked, but something about its structure indicated that behind this barrier lay the answer they had been searching for.

Rayan, a mixture of courage and nervousness in his steps, advanced and inserted the ancient key he had found in the box. The metallic sound of the lock turning echoed through the darkness, and with a slight effort, the door creaked open, revealing a shadowy space beyond. The owl entered without hesitation, as if it were familiar with what lay behind.

As they passed through the door, the group found themselves in an underground room, barely lit by the faint light coming through a small opening in the wall. The atmosphere was heavy, and the air felt dense, almost as if time itself had become trapped in this place.

Suddenly, a whisper broke the silence.

Ibai and Darío, two of their missing friends, were sitting on the floor, staring ahead as if they hadn't noticed their arrival. They appeared terrified and disoriented, as if they didn't know how they had ended up there. Their eyes were vacant, but there was something else in their gazes—something strange, as if they were not fully aware of what was happening around them.

The owl flew toward them and landed on a nearby table, observing them with an intensity that almost seemed to urge them to act. The group approached slowly, hearts racing.

Darío looked up at the sound of footsteps, but didn't seem to recognize them immediately. His expression was grim, as if trapped in some sort of trance.

— Darío? Ibai! Are you okay?! Noa cried, running toward them, tears in her eyes.

Ibai slowly lifted his head, but his words were distorted and disconnected, as if they came from far away.

— No... we're not... we're not complete... the cycle... it doesn't stop, Ibai murmured, his voice trembling.

Darío, like him, seemed trapped in a state of confusion, but his eyes glowed with a strange light, as if he were in another world, unable to see what was happening around him.

— The cycle...? What does that mean? Claudia asked, terrified. What happened to you, Darío? We've been looking everywhere!

Darío didn't answer immediately. Instead, the owl emitted a soft hoot, as if trying to get their attention. The sound seemed to resonate in the air, vibrating with mysterious energy. Suddenly, Darío blinked several times, as if waking from a deep sleep.

— The cycle... it consumes us, Darío said, his voice suddenly clear. It trapped us. It brings us here... to complete it. But if we don't stop it, everything will fall. You need to break it.

Rayan stepped forward, looking at Darío with a mixture of desperation and understanding. Something was happening, something that had been going on since the beginning. The cycle wasn't just a mystery of disappearances. It was something bigger, something that fed on trapped souls.

— How can we stop it? How can we save everyone? Rayan asked, almost pleading.

Ibai slowly lifted his head, and for a moment, his eyes seemed to return to reality.

— You must find the source. The root of it all. The darkness is there. Not in the basement, but under the stones of the school, Ibai said, in a low voice, as if he had had a sudden vision. Anastasia's soul still calls to those who come. The cycle continues because we haven't broken the chain.

Claudia, listening intently, tried to understand what they were saying. It was as if Darío and Ibai were trapped in a place between life and death, aware of something terrible that needed to be undone, but unable to act on their own.

— The chain...? The chain of what? Carolina asked, looking at the others. What chain?

Darío weakly raised a hand, pointing toward the wall where an old portrait hung, almost forgotten. It was the image of a mysterious woman, dressed in clothes from another era. Her face was enigmatic, but her eyes seemed to be staring directly at them.

— Anastasia... Darío murmured. It's her. The soul that cannot rest. She's trapped... along with us... until the cycle is complete.

Ibai nodded slowly.

— It's not just a mystery. It's a curse. And we... we are the ones who must break it.

The group looked at each other, the weight of Ibai and Darío's words falling on them like a yoke. Everything they had experienced, all the disappearances, everything that had happened at the school, wasn't an accident or coincidence. The cycle was connected to Anastasia's soul, and only they had the power to stop it.

The owl hooted again, as if urging them to act, not to waste any more time.

With their friends finally found but trapped in a trance, the group understood that they couldn't afford to lose any more time. The source of the cycle was closer than they had thought, and the fate of all of them depended on breaking the chain that bound the school's dark past to the present. But to do so, they would have to face the worst of what was hidden, what still lay buried deep within the place.

The owl flew toward the door, inviting them to follow.

The final step to break the cycle had begun.

CHAPTER 15: THE CLOCK

The owl flew toward the exit of the room, its wings beating softly, guiding them as always with a determination that could not be ignored. As the group moved closer, the air grew heavier, as if time itself was shifting around them. The light from the lamp flickered, casting unsettling shadows on the dust-covered walls. It was as though the owl knew something they didn't yet understand—something that would only be revealed if they followed its lead.

The owl led them down a narrow corridor, past the ancient doors of the basement. The silence was profound, interrupted only by the soft flapping of the bird's wings. Finally, they arrived at a large, circular room that seemed out of place inside the school. The walls were adorned with old clocks of various sizes, all showing the same time: twelve o'clock.

At the center of the room, on a stone pedestal, stood an enormous pendulum clock, its presence filling the space with an unsettling sense of urgency and mystery. Despite its age, the clock continued to function perfectly, its hands moving slowly, marking the passage of time with an eerie precision.

The owl perched on a shelf near the clock, watching the group with its large, penetrating eyes. It didn't take much to realize this was the key place, the central point of the entire mystery. The clock wasn't just an antique; it seemed to be the source of something deeper, a doorway to what had trapped them in this cycle of disappearances.

— This clock... it must be important, Rayan said, looking at the rest of the group. It's as if it marks the exact moment everything started.

Andrea cautiously approached the clock, examining the details of its structure. There were engravings on the base depicting various moments of the day. Each hour seemed to be linked to a significant event in the school's history.

Suddenly, Carolina pointed to something on the back of the clock. There, almost hidden from view, was a small slit in the wood, just beneath the face of the clock. It looked like the entrance to something concealed, something that had been waiting to be discovered.

— Look! There's something here, Carolina exclaimed, pointing to the slit.

With a determined gesture, Claudia stepped forward and slid her finger along the slit, feeling something move inside. A soft click resonated through the room, and with a near-magical motion, a small secret door at the base of the clock opened, revealing a small wooden box. The owl let out a soft hoot, as if the box was what they had been waiting for.

The group gathered around, watching in awe as Claudia lifted the box. The wood was carved with the same strange symbols they had seen on the map and in the basement. When they opened it, they found a small clock, almost identical to the one in the room, but with an inscription engraved on its surface:

Only when the clock stops, will the cycle begin to heal.

The message was clear, but also unsettling. The clock had to stop for something to change, something to unlock, but what would happen when they did? Were they ready for what would come next?

— This... this is what we need to break the cycle, right? Noa said, looking at the clock with a mix of fear and hope. We have to stop it. But how?

The sound of ticking from the other clocks in the room seemed to grow louder, as if all of them were synchronized with the central clock. The air was charged, and the owl, watching in silence, seemed to point toward the large pendulum clock.

Rayan was the first to approach, holding the small box in his hands. As he did, the ticking of the pendulum clock grew louder, its rhythm reverberating in their ears with increasing intensity.

— We have to do it now, Rayan said, bringing the small clock closer to the face of the large clock. Time is running out.

With a mixture of uncertainty and resolve, he placed the small clock on the base of the pendulum clock, right at the center of its face. The room trembled slightly, and suddenly, the clock began to slow.

The hands of the enormous clock, which had been moving without rest, began to decelerate. The ticking, which had filled the room, started to fade slowly. A deep silence took over the space.

Then, the room plunged into complete darkness, as if time had stopped at that precise moment. But in the air, there was a sense of release, as if the cycle that had kept everyone trapped was beginning to crumble. The owl flew toward the clock, landing in the center of its face, and let out a loud, clear hoot, as if it had fulfilled its purpose.

The group looked at each other in silence, unsure if what they had done was the right thing. Had they finally broken the cycle? Or was there something else left to do?

At that moment, the distant sound of a door opening echoed through the room. A new hidden door opened, and light began to filter through. Something had unlocked, and though the future remained uncertain, they knew that the clock had marked the end of the cycle and the beginning of a new opportunity.

— We did it, Carolina whispered, a relieved smile on her face.

But they knew there was still one final step. The truth behind everything that had happened in the school was closer than ever.

CHAPTER 16: THE KEY

The light that began to filter through the secret door illuminated the room with a soft, golden glow. The group, still processing what they had just experienced with the clock, approached the open door, sensing that the worst had passed, but the mystery was still unresolved. While the owl remained in place, watching them silently, something else caught Rayan's attention.

On the floor, near where the pendulum clock had been, something glimmered faintly. A metallic flash that seemed to reflect the light from the secret door. Rayan was the first to crouch down, feeling a strange pressure in his chest, as if the object was calling to him. When his hand touched the floor, a small metal key appeared before him. The key was old, but its design left no doubt: it was perfectly engraved with the same strange symbol they had seen on the box and the clocks.

— What is this? —asked Andrea, quickly approaching to examine it.

— It's a key... but it's not just any key —Rayan responded, not taking his eyes off the engraved figure. It seems to belong to something important. Something we haven't found yet.

Curious, Claudia approached the pedestal where the pendulum clock had been. She noticed that on one of the walls of the room, there was an ancient seal carved into the stone, almost imperceptible to the naked eye, as if it had been part of the original construction of the school. The seal was surrounded by strange symbols they didn't recognize, but somehow they seemed familiar. As if everything in this place was connected, like pieces of a puzzle.

— Could this be what Darío and Ibai were referring to? The seal... maybe it's what's controlling all of this —Claudia said, pointing to the symbol carved into the stone.

The group approached the seal, and when they looked more closely, they noticed something surprising: a slot at the bottom of the symbol, just the right size for the key to fit. The key seemed to have been made specifically for that purpose.

With a racing heart and trembling hands, Rayan stepped forward and placed the key into the slot. A deep click echoed in the room, as if something was waking up, and the seal began to glow. The stone slowly moved, revealing a hidden door that had been sealed for centuries.

The group took a step back, astonished and cautious. The owl, with its fixed gaze, seemed to give them the signal to move forward. The cycle had reached a critical point. Everything they had done up to now had led them to this moment. The ancient seal door was open, but beyond it lay an unknown path.

With a mix of fear and hope, the group decided to enter. The door creaked open, revealing a dark stone staircase that descended into the deepest parts of the school. The atmosphere grew denser, and the air smelled of dampness and antiquity.

— This must be the heart of it all —Mateo said, looking into the darkness at the end of the staircase. This is where we need to go. This is where it all began.

The owl, as if guiding them, flew ahead, heading into the darkness with a soft but determined flutter. The group followed in silence, knowing there was no turning back. Each of them felt the weight of the moment, but at the same time, there was a growing sense that they were finally about to discover the truth.

The staircase seemed endless, but eventually, they arrived at a large underground chamber. In the center of the chamber, a stone altar was covered in dust, and upon it, a large, ancient-looking book lay open. On its pages, strange drawings and words in an unknown language spread across, as if the book held forbidden knowledge, a very ancient secret.

The owl flew toward the altar and perched on the edge of the book, as if inviting them to read. Cautiously, Rayan approached and began to examine the pages, searching for something that would help them understand what was happening. And then, he found it.

On the central page, there was an illustration of a portrait of Anastasia, the figure that had been mentioned over and over again in their research. Around her face, the words read:

The seal that traps the soul, the key that unleashes destiny. Only those who open the seal will stop the eternal cycle.

— This is what we have to do —Rayan said, lifting his gaze from the book. The seal is not only trapping Anastasia, it's trapping the souls of everyone who has disappeared here. And now we know that we are the ones who must break it.

But there was a warning, one last line written in red, almost as if blood itself had marked the words:

To break the cycle, one must offer their soul to the seal. Only then will destiny be sealed.

A murmur of uncertainty rose among them. They knew they had reached the end, but they also understood that breaking the cycle could mean making a personal sacrifice, a very high price to pay to free everyone.

The owl watched them from its position on the altar, as if waiting for them to make their decision. They knew that their next step would determine not only their fate but the fate of everyone who had been trapped in the school and in the dark cycle of the past.

CHAPTER 17: THE PAST

The air in the underground chamber was thick, laden with centuries of secrets and forgotten whispers. Rayan, still holding the open book before him, felt a shiver run down his spine as the words about the sacrifice echoed in his mind. The cycle was about to break, but the price they had to pay was uncertain, and none of them knew exactly what to expect from what was to come.

Suddenly, the silence in the room was broken by a distant murmur, like a voice rising from the depths of darkness, as if the very past were claiming its place in the present. The owl, which had remained still until then, fluttered and flew toward the back of the chamber, perching on one of the rocky walls.

It was as though the owl was guiding them to something it had been waiting for a long time, as if its wings were whispering a message from the past.

Without thinking too much, Claudia stepped forward and touched the stone where the owl had perched. In that instant, a flash of blue light illuminated the room, and a series of images began to project onto the chamber's walls, like an ancient mural. The shadowed figures seemed to move, telling a hidden story.

The images showed the story of an old orphanage, built on the foundations of the same school where they now stood. The people who had lived there, the orphans who had grown up within those walls, the voices of children who had once been lost in the darkness of that place. Everything began to make sense.

The first face that appeared in the shadows was that of Anastasia, the woman they had heard about so many times. In the images, she was young, beautiful, with an enigmatic and sorrowful gaze. She didn't seem like just an ordinary orphan; she had a mysterious presence that the adults at the orphanage feared.

— Who was she really? —whispered Mateo, looking at the projections, which slowly faded only to be replaced by more memories.

The following images showed the orphanage at its peak, filled with children playing and running through the hallways, but there was something strange about their eyes, as if they were all trapped in some kind of spell. The workers of the place, the caregivers, wore vacant and heavy expressions, as though time did not pass for them.

Suddenly, the images shifted abruptly, showing the orphanage children disappearing one by one, as if something dark were claiming them. Some vanished completely, while others simply disintegrated into the air. The caregivers, who had initially seemed like authority figures, also began to show signs of suffering. It was as though everyone in that place had been absorbed by an evil presence.

One figure stood out among the rest: Anastasia. In the

final images, she was surrounded by shadows, her face distorted by pain and despair. Suddenly, Anastasia disappeared, but her soul seemed trapped in the walls of that place. It looked as though she had sealed something, something so dark and powerful that it had condemned all who came after her.

With a heartbreaking cry, Anastasia's image faded, and the seal on the stone wall began to glow, as if the presence of her soul had been released for a moment. The book in Rayan's hands also reacted, its pages beginning to turn unstable and blank, as though all the knowledge they had gathered so far was being replaced by the ultimate truth.

As the story of the past unfolded before them, a terrifying revelation became clear: Anastasia was not a victim, but a prisoner of her own fate. She had been chosen to guard the seal that held the curse, but at a terrible price. The cycle of disappearances, the shadows that haunted the school, the trapped spirits, everything that had happened, was connected to the fact that her soul had never been able to rest, and the seal had kept everything in balance.

Anastasia had offered her soul to maintain peace, but she had been deceived, and what seemed like a sacrifice to save others had become a cycle of endless suffering.

Claudia looked at her companions, her gaze fixed, understanding what was at stake.

— It's as if... Anastasia tried to seal everything forever. But something went wrong —she said, her voice trembling. She thought she was doing it for the children, but in the end... she herself got trapped.

Rayan nodded slowly, looking at the projections that were beginning to fade.

— All of this... the clock, the key, the seal... are pieces of a puzzle we haven't been able to solve until now. What happened in the past has followed us into the present. But if we break the cycle, everyone who's been trapped here, including us, will be freed.

But there was something more. As they watched the image of Anastasia trapped, one final vision appeared: Anastasia standing before them, with a pleading look, as if begging them not to repeat the same mistakes of the past.

— The price is high... —Anastasia's voice resonated in their minds, like a distant echo. The soul that breaks the cycle will be part of it, until someone else frees it. Only then will the cycle stop.

The past had spoken, and now the group understood what had to happen. Breaking the cycle, freeing Anastasia, meant making such a great sacrifice that the soul of the one who did it would remain trapped, until another came to take their place.

Time had stopped, but now the past and present intertwined. Who would be the one to make the final decision to end the curse and break the eternal cycle? Were they willing to make the necessary sacrifice to free everyone?

The fate of all depended on that answer.

CHAPTER 18: THE MIRROR

The atmosphere in the underground chamber grew even denser, as if the very walls were beginning to breathe in time with the ticking of the stopped clock. The group stood in silence, watching the last projections of the past, when a faint light began to glow in one corner of the room. Suddenly, a radiant gleam from a wall caught their attention. In that dark, almost hidden corner, there was something they had not noticed before: an ancient mirror, embedded in the wall, surrounded by carvings and strange symbols.

The mirror seemed out of place, as if it had been intentionally placed there, yet never seen before. It didn't reflect the faces of the group, nor the light that was beginning to filter into the chamber. Instead, the mirror showed a distorted image of the room, as if it were a vision from the past.

Rayan, curious but cautious, approached the mirror, feeling an invisible force drawing him towards it. The others followed, their hearts racing. As they drew closer, the shadows around the mirror seemed to deepen, as though an ancient power was beginning to awaken.

— This mirror... it doesn't reflect what's here, — Andrea said, her expression uneasy. It's like it's showing something... from another time.

The images in the mirror became clearer. On the surface, the hallways of the old orphanage appeared, exactly as they had been before the tragedy. Children playing, the caregivers in their places, but there was something strange about the reflected figures. Their eyes were empty, as if they were trapped in a trance, staring through the mirror without being able to escape.

It was then that Claudia noticed something even more disturbing. In the reflection, Anastasia suddenly appeared, standing before the mirror, her expression grim and sorrowful. Her eyes, though empty, seemed to be staring directly at the group.

— Look! —Claudia exclaimed, pointing at Anastasia's figure in the mirror. She's there... but she seems trapped, as if... as if she needs something.

The group fell silent, their hearts pounding. Anastasia seemed to be asking for something, something that only they could provide. As they watched, the pendulum clock in the other room began to move again, as if time itself were reactivating. At the same time, the mirror began to emit a blinding white glow, and a strange, whispering voice filled the room:

— The mirror... is the link. The sacrifice must be made before it. Only through the reflection of the soul can the cycle be freed.

The sound of the voice seemed to shake the walls of the underground chamber. The owl, which had remained silent until then, spread its wings and flew toward the mirror. With a quick turn, it perched on the surface of the glass, as if waiting for the group to make their decision.

Rayan, still trembling from the tension in the air, approached the mirror. He felt that there was something more than the words written in the book, something that could only be understood in front of the mirror. In the reflection, he could see Anastasia's figure, but now her eyes seemed clearer, more aware. She was watching them, and her lips moved slowly, as though speaking to them through the glass.

— To break the cycle, —Anastasia's voice clearly resonated in their minds now, one must look beyond what the eye can see. Only when the reflected soul is freed will time be restored. The sacrifice must be made with awareness, without fear, without regret.

A shiver ran through everyone's body. The group stared at the mirror, and it seemed that Anastasia was asking them to face their own reflection, to look deep into their souls, to understand if they were willing to pay the price to break the cycle.

Rayan stepped forward, resolute. He couldn't let Anastasia's story repeat, he couldn't allow more souls to remain trapped in that place, condemned to wander eternally. Anastasia had made her sacrifice, but they could end it. They could be the ones to free the curse.

— I'll do it, —Rayan said, his voice firm. I'll do it because we can't let this continue.

Rayan approached the mirror, looked at his own reflection, and saw himself as he was, but in his heart, he felt that something more was happening. The image in the mirror began to transform, the reflection of his face distorting, as though a part of his soul was being absorbed by the surface of the glass. He felt a strange energy fill his body, as though the mirror were claiming something from him.

The owl, perched on the edge, began to sing softly, a song that seemed to calm everyone's hearts, and the image of Anastasia in the mirror smiled, though with sadness. They knew what had to happen.

The shadow of the sacrifice began to take shape. Rayan extended his hand toward the mirror, and when his fingers touched the surface, the reflection shattered, but not into ordinary pieces. The mirror began to absorb the light, and a wave of energy swept through the room, bringing with it a cold wind that made the walls tremble.

At that moment, everything fell silent. The cycle had come to an end.

CHAPTER 19: THE CHANGE

When the mirror shattered into a thousand fragments of light and shadow, a profound change began to take place. Time no longer seemed to follow its usual course. The walls of the chamber trembled, and the air grew heavy, as if the atmosphere itself were trying to adjust to something that had never happened before.

Rayan, the first to touch the mirror, felt a pull in his soul, as if something inside him had loosened and begun to fade. But at the same time, a warm force enveloped him, a sense of liberation, as if the weight of centuries of curses and suffering was beginning to dissolve.

Suddenly, a figure materialized in the room. Anastasia appeared before them, but she was no longer the same shadow trapped in an endless cycle. Her face, once marked by despair, was now serene, almost peaceful. Her presence, once oppressive and dark, now radiated a soft light, as if she had finally found peace.

— You've done it, —Anastasia said, her voice vibrant but full of gratitude. The cycle... is over. I... I am no longer trapped.

The owl, which had remained at the edge of the altar, began to flutter softly, flying in circles around the room. It seemed to be celebrating, but also signaling that everything had changed. The chamber, which had until then been enveloped in a heavy, oppressive atmosphere, now seemed to breathe freely, as if the very energy of the place had been released.

The group exchanged looks, incredulous. They had accomplished the impossible: they had broken the cycle, and with it, freed the souls that had been trapped for so long by the curse. Anastasia was no longer a prisoner of her own fate.

— What happens now? —Claudia asked, her voice full of awe.

Anastasia looked at her and smiled faintly.

— Time... will no longer be the same. The cycle is broken, but the world you know will not be the same. The souls that were trapped, those who disappeared here, are free now. And you... you have changed something within yourselves. The balance has been restored, but you must continue on your journey.

The group felt a slight pressure in the air, as if a heavy burden had been lifted from their shoulders, but at the same time, something new was beginning to form. They didn't know if everything had truly ended, if the story had really come to a close, or if now they themselves would be the new guardians of the mystery that had been hidden for so long.

The school, which now seemed more at peace, began to change around them. The walls, once aged and covered in shadows, seemed to have regained their original light, as if the darkness that had surrounded them for so long had been dissipated. In the distance, through the windows, they could see the landscape bathed in the glow of a bright dawn.

But something lingered in their minds, an unanswered question. Though Anastasia had been freed, the idea that there was a deep connection between the past and the present made them wonder if everything they had experienced was merely the beginning of something even greater.

— What do we do now? —Rayan asked, looking at his friends and then at Anastasia.

Anastasia, with a serene gaze, gave them one last answer.

— What you do now... is return to your time. The story of this place will never be forgotten, but you must move forward. The door you have opened is not just the one that closed the cycle, but the one that will guide you toward new adventures. But do not forget what you have learned: the balance between the past and the present must always be maintained.

The owl, flying toward them, seemed to be the final sign that everything had ended. Anastasia slowly faded, becoming a soft light that dissolved into the air.

The group, now aware of their new role, took a step back. The chamber, the mirror, the seal — everything had ceased to be a place of darkness and fear. It was now a place of transformation, renewal, and liberation.

With one last look at the place where everything had begun, the group turned and left the chamber. As they ascended the stairs, the weight of the answers began to settle on them. They knew that, although the curse had been broken, the school remained a special place, holding secrets that only a few could understand. The past no longer haunted them, but the story of that place would remain in their memories.

The future, now open before them, shone with possibilities.

CHAPTER 20: THE RETURN

When the group left the underground chamber, the sense of liberation they had experienced still resonated in their hearts. The school, now filled with a renewed warmth, seemed to have healed in some way. The walls, once oppressive and burdened with a dark history, were now bathed in the light of the new day. The atmosphere had changed, not just in the physical space but in their own spirits as well.

Despite everything they had gone through, one question still lingered in their minds: What about Eduardo? The teacher who, though he had been part of their doubts and suspicions throughout the story, had also guided them toward the resolution of the mystery. The group made their way to the classroom, where they knew he would be waiting.

When they entered the room, they saw Eduardo sitting at his desk, looking out the window with a thoughtful expression. He seemed absorbed in his own thoughts, but when the group entered, he lifted his gaze with a slight smile, as if everything were under control.

— Ah! You're back, —he said, his voice calm, almost relaxed. Ready to continue with the day?

The group exchanged glances, but something in the air had changed. The tension that had once existed between them and Eduardo seemed to have dissipated, though the questions that troubled them still remained.

Did he know what had happened? Was he aware of the sacrifice they had all made to free the trapped souls?

Rayan was the first to speak, looking at Eduardo with a mixture of confusion and curiosity.

—Teacher... did you know what was going on? Did you know what lay behind all of this?

Eduardo watched them for a moment, and a sincere smile appeared on his face, though there was also a shadow of sadness. He slowly stood up and walked toward the blackboard, as if trying to organize his thoughts before speaking.

— I knew something... but not everything. This place has a deep history, a history that few know, and even fewer should know, —he said, his voice sounding more serious. Since I arrived at this school, I felt that there was something more. Something dark, something incomplete. But I never imagined what was really happening here, nor what you all had to face.

The group looked at him in silence, listening attentively. Eduardo continued, his tone more reflective.

— I'm not a stranger to the forces that reside in this place. Like you, I've been an involuntary participant in this cycle. Like the caretakers of the old orphanage, some of us have become trapped without knowing how to break it. The mystery of Anastasia has been larger than any of us could understand.

The group was starting to understand. Eduardo wasn't a villain, but he wasn't completely unaware of the school's history either. He had been part of a greater cycle, one in which, unknowingly, he had become involved.

— So...? —Claudia began. Was it just a coincidence that we were the ones who ended up solving it all? How did you know we had to find the mirror? Or the seal?

Eduardo lowered his gaze, and for a moment, he seemed to hesitate.

— I didn't know everything. But... there were signs. In this place, the energies are ancient, and over time, one begins to notice patterns. The owl that guided you... it wasn't just an animal, but an entity that had always been watching, waiting for the right moment to act. Anastasia, her trapped soul, never wanted what happened, but she knew the cycle had to be broken one day.

Eduardo took a deep breath and turned toward the group, his expression now serious.

— What I couldn't stop, what I never knew how to fully prevent, was the fact that the past always returns. This place, its secrets, are always waiting to be discovered by those strong enough to face them.

A sense of relief began to fill the room. Though Eduardo's answers didn't clarify everything, they allowed the group to understand his role in the events that had taken place. He had not been the enemy, nor an innocent bystander. He had been someone who, like them, had been part of something much larger.

— And now what? —Andrea asked, looking at Eduardo with a mixture of hope and caution.

The teacher smiled gently and approached the window, looking out at the school grounds, which now seemed calmer and filled with light.

— Now, what remains is to live with the knowledge of what has happened here. This place has many stories, but the most important thing is that you are free. The cycle has been broken, and though we won't be able to forget what occurred, we can move forward.

Rayan nodded, and the others did too, feeling that although the answers were not complete, there was no longer room for doubt and distrust. The mystery that had shrouded the school, the terror that had marked their experience, had been resolved. But with that came a new understanding: the past could not be undone, but it could be understood.

The bell rang, signaling the start of another class, and though the group of friends could not forget what they had lived through, they knew that now they could return to the routine, with a new perspective on the school, on Eduardo, and on themselves.

As they headed to their desks, Eduardo looked at them

with a slight smile.

— Welcome back to class, kids. The future is in your hands now.

And though the echo of the lost voices from the past still resonated in the shadows of the school's history, the future no longer seemed so dark.

The Echo of the School

CHAPTER 21: ECHOES OF THE PAST

The day continued with an unusual calm at the school, as if the very air had changed in density. The kids sat at their desks, but something still lingered deep in their minds. The echoes of the past resonated in their hearts, as if the walls of the school, now restored to their former beauty, still held secrets waiting to be uncovered.

Although the cycle had been broken and the dark presence that had haunted them for so long had disappeared, the kids couldn't help but wonder if everything had truly come to an end.

Despite Eduardo's words and the sense of peace surrounding them, there was something more—an elusive presence, something they couldn't explain, but which seemed to be everywhere, in every corner of the school.

Suddenly, Noa looked up and stared out the classroom window. The air was strangely still, but her gaze fixed on something that shimmered in the distance, near the old gardens, a place they never usually visited.

— Do you see it? —Noa said, nervously pointing at the window. — Over there, by the trees... something's shining.

The others looked, but they couldn't see anything clearly. Only the empty garden, fallen leaves, and the immense tranquility that still enveloped everything. However, the feeling that something else was happening grew stronger in their hearts.

Eduardo, who had been observing carefully, slowly turned toward them. His face, though calm, showed an expression that suggested he, too, sensed something strange.

— The echoes of the past never truly disappear, —he said in a grave tone. — This place has a long history, and scars don't heal immediately.

Samuel frowned and stood up from his seat.

— What do you mean by that? We thought everything was over... that Anastasia was free.

Eduardo looked at the kids, but his eyes carried a somber understanding.

— What you've done is free the trapped souls. But the echoes of the past are more than memories... they are presences that have been here too long. Though the souls of the children are now at peace, the school remains a place of memory. Sometimes, the past seeks to return.

The room filled with a heavy silence. The kids looked at one another, searching for answers, trying to understand the teacher's words.

It was then that the owl, which had been nearby, took flight again, and a soft whisper floated through the air. The group turned toward it, and the figure of the bird seemed to be guiding them toward the door.

Rayan, with his heart racing, felt that the owl was showing them something more. Without thinking too much, he stood up and left the classroom, followed by his friends. Eduardo watched them from the window with a worried look, but he said nothing. He knew that, no matter how much he tried to keep them inside the four walls of the classroom, something had been awakened in them. Something that connected them to the past.

The owl flew ahead, heading toward the back garden of the school, where the air seemed heavier, and the trees, though beautiful, gave a sense of antiquity. As they drew closer, the group could see what the owl had been indicating: an old stone on the ground, half hidden by the underbrush.

With their hearts pounding, the kids approached. Layna was the first to crouch down and move the dry leaves covering the stone. When she uncovered it completely, she saw that there was an inscription carved into its surface, very old, with symbols that seemed to glow with an inner light.

— This... we've never seen this before, —Layna murmured, touching the stone cautiously. — It seems like some kind of seal.

Mateo bent down to read the engraving:

The past does not die, it hides, waiting for the moment when the brave will face it again. Those who have been touched by darkness will always carry its light.

The kids felt a chilling revelation as they read those words. What did they mean? Had the past truly never disappeared completely?

In that moment, a gust of wind blew through the trees, and the echo of distant voices could be heard in the distance, as if they were being called by something else—something that connected them to the events of long ago.

Rayan, with a sense of urgency in his chest, looked at his companions.

— We can't stay here. We need to go back inside the school. Something else is happening.

The group nodded in silence. Even though the cycle had ended, the fact that the past never truly disappeared haunted them, and they knew something else was awakening.

As they returned to the school, the atmosphere felt strange. The lights flickered at times, and the echo of distant footsteps resonated in the old stairs of the hallway. The kids made their way toward the classroom, but when they entered, something was wrong. The place seemed distorted in some way. The desks were farther apart than usual, and a light mist seemed to envelop the room.

On the blackboard, something had been written in white chalk: "The past does not forgive, but sometimes, the future must accept its burden."

Eduardo, who had entered with them, stopped dead in his tracks when he saw the words written on the board.

— Did you... write this? —he asked, his voice trembling.

The group looked at each other, unsure of how to respond. No one had touched the board.

Then, a cold wind swept through the classroom, and the owl that had guided them appeared again in the window, watching them with an intense gaze.

The past never dies.

THANK YOU FOR READING THIS BOOK.